ESSENTIAL POETS SERIES 164

Canada Council for the Arts — Conseil des Arts du Canada

Guernica Editions Inc. acknowledges the support of the Canada Council for the Arts.

JOHN OUGHTON

TIME SLIP

GUERNICA
TORONTO – BUFFALO – LANCASTER (U.K.)
2010

Antonio D'Alfonso, editor
Guernica Editions Inc.
P.O. Box 117, Station P, Toronto (ON), Canada M5S 2S6
2250 Military Road, Tonawanda, N.Y. 14150-6000 U.S.A.

Distributors:
University of Toronto Press Distribution,
5201 Dufferin Street, Toronto (ON), Canada M3H 5T8
Gazelle Book Services, White Cross Mills, High Town, Lancaster LA1 4XS U.K.

First edition.
Printed in Canada.

Legal Deposit – Second Quarter
Library of Congress Catalog Card Number: 2009931513
Library and Archives Canada Cataloguing in Publication
Oughton, John, 1948-
Time slip / John Oughton. — 1st ed.
(Essential poets series ; 164)
Poems.
ISBN 978-1-55071-302-2
I. Title. II. Series: Essential poets series ; 164
PS8577.U34H48 2009 C811'.54 C2009-904142-1

Contents

Introduction

What is the point of poetry? Although it has been in some times and places a popular art, it is not so today, in the technologically-driven twenty-first century. It is hard for a single voice or vision, however accomplished, to compete with the blandishments of hundreds of TV channels, millions of websites, and all the other distractions. It also offers at best a frail claim to immortality – patterns of words are flimsy bulwarks against the expanses of time and space within which individual lives flare.

Yet people still take the time to write, read and listen to poetry. Perhaps that is because it comes from an ancient human impulse to praise, evoke, and rail against powers greater than our own. Or perhaps it is because poetry is in some ways a multi-media art: even though it appears a verbal structure, it calls upon sound, imagination, memory, senses, and thought. Because poetry can take any form and draw energy from almost any theme, it is as protean as the human race itself. Since I began writing it in high school, I have taken occasional sabbaticals during which I wrote little; but poetry has always called me back with another challenge.

This collection spans work written over more than thirty years. I have never been a prolific poet. While I admire those who can emit a book of publishable poetry every year, that is not my way. Rather, my oyster requires a lot of sand and several months to produce a single pearl. Each of my four books came from a different publisher, and the time between them ranged from eleven to four years. Thus, most who have read my poetry are familiar with only one or two books. Here is a chance for poems from different times, places and on many themes to meet in the same room.

Despite repeated efforts, I could not convince my scanner to convert the earlier books into editable text. So I have retyped the poems myself, which led to a very pragmatic editorial rule-of-thumb: is this poem worth the work of retyping it? If not, I left it out. This approach also favoured shorter poems over the longer ones. One would hope that I have learned some things about the art of poetry over these decades, but I have kept changes to the poems to a minimum, focusing on improvements to punctuation, line and stanza breaks.

My first book was *Taking Tree Trains*, published at Coach House Press in 1973 under the editorial eye of Victor Coleman. I had a family connection to the press, as my sister Libby had worked there (and did the press work to produce this slim volume). I worked at Coach House myself in the early 1970s as a summer intern and then for a full year as a typesetter/editor/travelling salesman. The book's design was by rick/simon, and I typeset the poems myself on an IBM Selectric typewriter with its high-technology removable golfball font. This small collection included poems written the previous year when I attended Irving Layton's poetry workshop at York University (my classmates included Ken Sherman). The title inevitably led to some enjoyable confusions. One library listed the book as *Talking* Tree Trains, while another was convinced that it is Taking *Three* Trains.

My next book took eleven years to mature. I continued to write poetry, on and off, and circulate various versions of the manuscript that eventually was accepted by Mosaic Press as *Gearing of Love* (the title is taken from a line translated from "The Aleph" by Jorge Luis Borges: "I saw the gearing of love and the modifications of death"). I was fortunate that Mosaic's poetry editor at the time was Ken Sherman, who applied his own fine poet's sense to the selection and improvement of the poems. One irony about this collection is that I had originally circulated it as illustrated by my own black and white photographs. When more than one prospective publisher politely rejected it while adding "We prefer to choose our own art work," I removed the photographs. When Mosaic accepted the then purely text collection, the publisher asked innocently: "Is there any art work you'd like to add to this collection?" So the photos went back in.

This collection reflects some significant events in my life since 1973: the six months I spent in Japan inspired the first section, while the death of my sister Cathy, the estrangement of my father from our family, and other life events coloured the rest of it. It also used a wider poetic pallette than my first book, veering from serious (even borderline-sentimental) love poems to political, comic, and ironic ones. One of the latter poems perhaps still requires a subtext: when I wrote "Depression," I was considering my own, somewhat self-indulgent, use of that emotional state, not mocking those with serious or clinical depression.

Once *Gearing* was completed, I found myself seized by an obsession. Somehow, I became convinced that my next book would be written from the viewpoint of a historical woman: the dancer, sometime spy, and courtesan Mata Hari. I researched her life, consuming biographies, wildly inaccurate movie versions, and other material as I could find it. Why I was so drawn to her story, I still don't know. Perhaps she represented my feminine side, or anima; perhaps I was simply drawn by the fact that the French secret service had recorded her account of her life, but then put it under a seal of secrecy for one hundred years (not due to expire until 2017!). So the poems in *Mata Hari's Lost Words* (catalogued by more than one library as *Last Words*) reflect, inevitably, my own quirks and style, but do attempt to create a distinct voice for my version of Mata Hari. Some of the poems were performed as a one-act, one-woman play at Acadia University in 1988-1989. Although I was taken to task by a few reviewers for even attempting to write from a woman's viewpoint, I still feel this is my most fully realized collection. Again, my sister Libby, as a patron saint of Canadian publishing, had a hand: she was then running Ragweed Press in PEI, and accepted the collection. Richard Lemm was its scrupulous editor.

My fourth book, *Counting Out the Millennium*, also marks my first international publication. In the infancy of the Internet, I had joined an email list of people interested in creative writing. This list, called CREWRT-L (for Creative Writing in Education for Teachers and Students) was founded by Eric Crump, then at the University of Missouri. While we discussed creative writing practice and pedagogy, we also shared samples of our work. Eventually a list member from Texas, Palmer Hall, asked if I had any manuscripts he might consider for his new press, Pecan Grove. Since Canadian publishers at the time seemed too overbooked to consider my work, I sent him the poems that eventually became *Counting*. The title is meant to play a double role, both in counting down the years until 2000, and discounting some of the millennial hysteria that followed (remember Y2K? My God, all the computers will blow up!). The poems themselves reached into some new realms, both forward into more obvious experimentation with language and form, and backwards into my past and memories. A few of them were written, or improved, while I attended the summer Jack Kerouac School of Disembodied Poetics at Boulder Institute in Boulder, Colorado (where I was fortunate enough to work with William Burroughs, Allen Ginsberg, Anne Waldman, Robert Duncan, and others).

Since that collection appeared in 1997, I have continued to write new poems. The best of these are included here. A selection of these appeared in 2002 as the chapbook *Take With You What You've Left* by my own micro-press, Sixth Floor Press. The press's name pays homage to an advanced poetry group I've had the pleasure of facilitating during the past several years. We originally met on the sixth floor at Toronto's Ontario Institute for Studies in Education, and when a founding group member, retired, we moved to the fifth-floor cafeteria. I need to thank several present and former members of the group – Clara Blackstock, Rosemary Blake, Merle Nudelman, Ruth Roach Pierson, Patria Rivera, Mary Lou Soutar-Hynes, Sheila Stewart, Elana Wolff – for their editorial assistance with many of these poems, and their reminding me through their own commitment, that poetry is worth taking seriously.

So here are selections representing more than three decades of poetry. I hope that you like at least some of them.

To my daughter Eireann,
and in grateful acknowledgement of the support and suggestions of the Long Dash writing group: Rosemary Blake, Clara Blackwood, Merle Nudelman, Mary Lou Soutar-Hynes, Sheila Stewart, Elana Wolff

History = His Story (Olson)

I wake at four in the morning
exact mate and anti-hour to day
twelve hours and twice those years after my start
that far from mothers this far into music
Hour of the fat jackal whining
as it dines the street of our marvellous garbage
greater and shinier trash than Shakespeare knew
Thirst clanging mouth wound
up by the night's birthday drinks
Water I cry
that far from my first phoneme
which won me applause of rubber
gloves on my buttocks shiny
as pearls. Both sound – slap –
and shape – round – now nesting
inside two dozen Chinese puzzle boxes
each built to last a year
and
never finished for
that reason

In sleep I tap
I tap them for tuned skulls, is
this my own life now or
do I begin at
the end of this phrase?
Alone in a room the offwhite of
my mind's 1948 hospital
I nurse unacted desires
that much of the child

yet turns within me
preferring dreams for mother milk
and I wake thirsty for
water or this – turn
this hour of echoes B side of the disc
B for beginnings

Trees Two

Were you a tree
would you bend
sway, drink
know the earth
thru long toes
sail white curves
for all winter
and greet spring
forthcoming with soft
green applause

Inner Springs

We walking on ice the way
a cat on piano keys walks
over glazed mice in a dream

Mousey squeaks between the
writhing Swiss cheese blocks
of lakeside ice – listen

Did you hear that theme
Crazy Katachurian
Mickey Mussorgsky

warmth creeps around
the hyp not ized ice
like a cat on piano keys

with something else
on its mind's cateye
spring love or us

That Line

I turn my life upside down
nothing falls out. No change
in the pockets of this train
six sprockets the head's projector
unreels, grinding land through
as if a pocket of change lay ahead
someone tied to the rails
yellowed 1920's steam somehow missing
her, the frame of a movie I do
not appear in. My head bulging
with the alternation of ideas
like a light bulb. And then

My life hanging by its threaded foot
from the ceiling nothing falls
like a hardwood tree opening its
valentine spectrum
for the leaden skies come
This train projects you expecting me
like a pine resin's song rising
through the year the winds rising
cry salute the crystal fist of winter
from which nothing falls

This train the switch
connects us drifting unverbed until
the poem is ripe, our arms frame
each other. Our pockets drop from us
with the weight of living
a long line between us you

a light through those trees life
sometimes flies into, and words
taking another track
over rivers full of fall

Training

This train a short sentence
    not of thought
        stammers a long line over white snow pages
like some unlovely gray ship
    it tears between standing wave drifts
        only the moon measures, opens
a bow wave in the closing sea
    of perspective
but sight tows a zipper that shuts
    the gap of where we were

Inside, a child wakes: the train
    with its jumping seats and important noises
        is still absurdly in the same place he is
a narrow night fogged city
    much like the city he left in
        that other today before sleep. Awake
he sits still in his swaying seat
Crossings understand the train
    They wave arms cluck lights bell the night
        and cut the traffic that isn't there
    in deference to the scar the train
stitches over mooning white drifts

The train's in a hurry to join city to
city since perspective is nip-
ping at its tail (smaller
when longer) so it
stammers the same
line to the
listening
land

Life in Forest Hill

Here at the confluence
of Forest and Hill
our Cadillac-driving neighbours never wave
in their flow to Bay St.
and below the landlord roars
like a diesel bus at his brood
"Today is tomorrow! I'll give you
something to remember!"
– Proust militant
overhead the sky thinks dimly
of sun's elsewhereabouts

In vision at night
the bagel triumphant rises above
the sleeping streets like Ezekiel's wheel
and everyone dreams tomorrow to be
the same

God's Best Poems

In the beginning was the word
light and all life
woke to the whisper
of winged names
So vast a poem demanded
applause
Adam was spelled from
the dumb clay, Eve
rhymed of his rib
but the serpent
who sang more subtly
showed how loudly
their unambiguous flesh
rang through the hosannas
banished

Later men began a sonnet
that might tower until
it signed the bright page
of the heavens. God
broke the verse with a
hammer of strange tongues
Babel. Human prayers still
praise that divine surrealism
as, smoky and supplicant, they
float skyward, each asking
for the word

Back Again – For Mary

Forgetting for you
the history of your back
with my fingers was
remembering the waves
we once made there
and walking a beach
while the tide leaves
irrevocably
the stars which
from sea view don't change
but neither can I caress them
Your hair breaks over smooth reefs
swamping my word fleets
in their quest for old harbours

Que voulez-vous, masseur
but the touch of flowers
and a back unabstract
to write such ravings on

For Jan Apart

I flick the switch
that turns on darkness
climb aboard my bed
but lightning's digit
prods the sky insane again
rain I think of the web
of our lives together stretched
a strand across dew-jeweled shrubs
distance walks between. I don't
sense you swimming in dreams
green or flying the kite
of your bright art on
the images singing through
your brain thunder
slams down on my thoughts
and a whole other weather
breathes around you. I wonder
how you wake without me
faking an alarm to see
what you've caught in dreams
away from me mysterious
in night obscure so much
moves between us changing

I Am an Elephant And

clumsy among love's flowers in
my wrinkled habits grey

but you make me feel
my trunk's a flute and
four legs drum for your dance

Graduation Advice from Old Japan

Take rocks
for text
learn stream's
tongue well

Touch moss, method
of philosopher tombs
Slow as knowledge
it befurs shade

and stone. Walk on
the legs discourse
overlooks. Leave that lyre
in the wind a while

like King David's
When time accepts you
listen to its song
until it's your own

For Yuan Mei

(18th century Chinese poet)

Almost another
birthday. I drink
coffee and reflect
on the hill, how
the pines transmute
it to sky
and clouds with
their small, high
heads floating
As a brush
sublimes stone
and water to song

Kyoto, December 6

Foreign

In Kyoto's Botany Gardens
plum blossom of improbability pink
how strange I must seem

beard like a brush that quit
painting and eloped with the ink
old coat out of season, a pet

dog's pelt. The natives are newly
dressed, their faces as clear as
advertisements. My being's a challenge

to which "Hurro!" is the response
Foreign status make me as crazy
as I am, with all my homes

spiralled on my back
Alien, exile, tourist, tramp
Almond eyes seek the nut I am

Taizo-In Rock Garden, Kyoto

He is alone in
the ancient garden
of stone and sand
with a waterfall for each ear
the moon is a perfect
half-coin of silver
high in the blue sky
sun warms the eye
with late-day gold
the air is cold
carp chorus
gold and silver below the mirror
of the still pond

At the half, he hears both words
and the sound in the heart
of a large stone: that one
there, the perfectly-raked
gravel waves echoing it
the air has the precision
of a poem and he is half sick
for home, half hungry for the strange
this moon riding an afternoon sky
this garden which to itself so wisely tends
people and praise seem
exotic, one-day-a-year blooms

Donald Duck in Quebec

Donald and Daisy chastely part at her door
although they quack lover's French and
have gone out together these thirty years
Donald always buying le film et popcorn
Daisy not forgetting les burgers après

O wondrous ducks in your bows
shirts and shoes but never pants
is sex determined by who pays
and afterwards drives that car
like a fendered rabbit hutch
Is Disney in a cryogenic trance
stirred by slow nitrogen dreams
of dating humanimals drawn by ghost hands
forging Walt across the world

Burger-loving ducks in flatfooted fables
who think in amphibious joual
tell us what beasts we be

The Elephant Man Who Looked Perfectly Normal

For Ken Sherman

No one was fascinated, repelled
or howled at him as inhuman
but with all that time and not a thing
to do or think, the roughness of his brain
grew rusty. Roughness
had worn down too many days
that held him in them
how his tusks waned as the moon shaved him clean
so far from the sweet grass of the savannas

When women neared, they sniffed on him failure
and clattered away like the clogs of nuns
the elephants trumpeted Taps in his ears
with lyrics that went, "Brother
the poachers have you too"
And although he looked perfectly normal
through the lens of his eye
people could glimpse elephants dying
their tusks becoming piano keys and cameos
as their heavy bodies fell

My Niece Becomes

She becometh pure
flower and perfume
so all the buzzing male bees
bumble up in cars
to ask if you're the kind
that opens at night

Even the tired, safe-seeming
married drone you've know for years
appears thick with imagined pollen to say
he loves his big bike more than his wife
and she, bitchy from drinking vanilla
threw away its key

Sixteen and blossomed
you skip across the potato fields
your fair hair lifted by the sea-wet wind
leaving the male bees behind
like the brown bottles they heave from their cars
and they shrug and swear and go back
to the same old clover patch they know

Lady`s Fan Poem

For Joni Mitchell

A diamond sings through a long
black snail of vinyl
vain and venal life seems
until the guitar warms and
shores up hearts. Nerves node
and chords cross fingers
to catch that delicate feeling

It's lonely when the big lights
blare and fans come on for old tracks
how many revolutions ago
but the songs keep moving closer
almost at your shoulder when you brush
your long Saskatoon hair

The strings catch colours
and light little blazes in the multipliers
telling the world her secrets
and how well they fit
all the ears out there

Rimbaud

Rimbaud
spun words
from his tongue like clay birds
then shot them up
At nineteen
fired poetry
for slight to hand and aim.
Ballistic
ran guns to Africa
until his leg fell off

Problem

I have dreams of violence
but my poems are painfully polite

Salvation Army, help me fight
my way out of this paper bag

until I hear the fog horns sirens howl
across this city deep in sleep
until all the cows come home
with seven-foot tall Masai warriors
milking them of blood

Depression

One thing about it is you're never bored
because what you've got is so much worse it's
almost interesting and you can always think about it
in fact you're almost hot for another
laying on of the hand
that pushes you down and down

All things attain equal significance
a license plate read with
the same attention you give to poetry
Even while writing this you're
Being Depressed. Your head is detached
and volleyed across the net between
self-hate and self-pity
and the score is love, one, set

Why not pick up this typewriter
and bash that head with it until
the letters you thought would explain it all
stand out all over your skin
a literary tattoo where people read
what they want? As illegible as the
mask you perfect, showing no feeling

Throughout these charades you stink of normal
but the black hovering shapes in your brain
smell what's there and wait

Have a nice day

For My Dead Sister

We sit together, staring at coals
in the fireplace of the home where
we grew up. My sister tells me
that she'll be cremated
would have given
science her body but now
"no one wants it"

Thirty-one, cancer
And she is somehow calm, seems
at that point where life and death are equally
visible, neither cloaked by desiring
she says the only thing she regrets
is not being able to see her two
blonde daughters grow

November. Hesitant snow drifts as she
could go, in a month. But right now
staring at coals
she is a flame from which the candle
wanes

Waiting to See My Father

His voice on the phone fills me
with who he is
I don't know what to say
he's seventy-one, just divorced
gone for years. His shock
of hair white as a
baby's conscience
name still the same as my own

We're strangers with a lot in common
unsure how much to admit
I feel him surface in my distance
abstraction, coldness to whoever loves me
but my gifts I take for my own
we talk about photography and travel
anything but who we are

We never learned the comfort
of silence together. Nor do we fish
follow hockey, or even have cars
to compare. Between us is the filter
of what remains
when father and son
have left. We still hold
each other inside – men who don't know
the secret of how to nurture
and release

In Memory of Drummer Larry Dubin

Energy is eternal delight.
William Blake

You played what you heard
and opened patterns of city sound
for us: a door slam, car honk and elliptical offbeat
of Coke can wind-rolled down the gutter
once linked by you became necessary
as the riffs of machines running, rain
sounding out junk on a rooftop, shoes
descending a wooden staircase
all this ran through the dancing
fabric your stick wove from the drums
in French *la batterie*, because some
stick/struck/strokes
kicked the band along like volts up the spine
and then you'd brush a whisper to barely
cross the capacitance of ears

In your hands the maple exclamation marks
spelled a sphere that became chord and centre
to what anyone else was playing
Tom-tom, tambour, tambourine, traps
hi-hat, snare, bass, cymbal, blocks
With these in your mind you kept time
even while listening, making silence
the backbeat of your heart

Now what marches behind your silence
is a New Orleans jazz funeral of sounds

varying step enough to show they dance
because they take and shape and
give back time, and never quite repeat
they are your riffs

Mariners

The smell of your skin
lingering on my skin
the moan of foghorns through the night
and our immersion in each other
make me imagine a ship
on which everyone, even the captain
is drunk on love and whiskey
and the horn toots torch songs
as the ship steams up Main Street
the bow curling pavement back exactly
along the dotted line
parking meters and astonished cops
are thrown back like herring in the wake
floating in our little bed
we do not hear it bearing down on us

but come to on different continents
and all I hear of you is gulls screaming
all you hear of me
is the sound of a ship's jazz band
swallowed by the sea

Sand to Glass

Those bottles we throw
to the ocean hold
a message for us

lean your ear to my mouth
the siren sang
man's alchemy burns
sand to glass the seas
turn glass to sand

Zero Aperture, Photographer

After reading *Yeats, the Tarot and the Golden Dawn*
by Kathleen Raine, and *The Negative* by Ansel Adams

The number Zero is a Fool
an empty O under glass
who seeks more in a scene
but what is, is
the Fool is bottomed in bells
which strike against
the rained grass
a little dog named Dark
dogs his heels

When the sky blasts light
his index finger will twitch
up ahead, where he does not look
the cliff ends. Like a shutter
he will trip
and instead catch his foot
on the living tree which
gives off light
upsydaisy down

Note: In a traditional "analogue" camera, the aperture number states how much light the lens will admit in a given time – the lower the number, the more light. An aperture of zero is impossible.

Mata Hari

Margaretha Gertruuida Zelle was born in the northern Dutch region of Friesland. She met and married a military officer, Rudolph MacLeod, through a "companion wanted" ad, and accompanied him to Java. There she became intrigued by Javanese culture, especially its music and dancing. She left her abusive husband, moved to Paris, and began a new career as a circus performer, artist's model, and then Oriental dancer under the stage name Mata Hari (Javanese for "Eye of Dawn"). Eventually she became one of Europe's leading courtesans, women noted not only for their erotic skills, but also for their beauty, wit and sense of style – they were the tabloid pop stars of their day.

Then came World War I. Multilingual, from a neutral nation, and intimate with powerful men from various nations (Berlin's Chief of Police, the Prince of Wales, French officers, a young Russian pilot), she fell under suspicion. She was arrested as a spy in France at a time when the war was not going well for the Allies, and convicted on rather flimsy evidence. At 40, she was executed by a firing squad in 1917; her only surviving child also died young and tragically. Her memoirs, dictated from jail to a journalist/friend, were ordered sealed for 100 years and remain, largely untouched, in French military archives.

The Goat-Cart

A child lives in a kaleidoscope
Each turn of the planet
juggles known faces, shards of
colour in new combinations
The first memory I have of standing
apart from the tumbling shards
is my sixth birthday and I'm the windfall
apple of my father's eye
plump and formal, puffing a cigar
he might buy me the world
but settles on two prancing goats
and the tiny cart with me
as queen, goddess, charioteer
urging them on
no other father in Leeuwarden so extravagant
no other mother would let her daughter drive

The town snoozes in midday sun
my goats' eyes as opaque as Satan's

My steeds prance along dusty streets
a man swears as I almost run him down
two little girls playing hopscotch
freeze and stare at me in fear
This rush of speed
makes me icon, figurehead
who does not move
though my long dark hair flails the wind

What this memory gives me
knowing I can ignore my fear
plunge into speed as if it were all I wanted
all anyone will see of me
the shining eyes
the recklessness

As a woman, dancing, I use the delicacy
of sharp hooves racing over cobblestones
as the world rushes toward me, I learn to stand
unmoved

After Mother`s Funeral

I play this piano
atone for her death
my mother mourned only by her family
our pride broken in public
now privately interred

my fingers between the white keys
skull teeth, ivory grave fence
black stone notes that end
broken

I play nothing, and jam down the sustain pedal
so the piano hums its own threnody

the perennial favourite
unfinished sonata of the newly alone
child whose mother has gone into
a dark cleft spaded in the earth
her only faithful suitor, death

ashes to ashes, dust to dust
only truth in that lie of
a funeral service

I assemble the triad
my father's pride, disgrace
abandoning of us, shade it with
the minor note of losing part of myself

my right hand gathers grief and
shards it into the future

my left grasps my mother's pain
and roots it in earth

This piano is the silence my mother
becomes
the silence my fingers ripple and still
an instrument of the dead
ivory stripped from elephants
wood cloven from trees

Three final notes
launch it as her funeral barge

I swear when I die no one will forget me
so easily. I play the piano
to obliterate all this
then let the lid slam onto my hands

Rendezvous at the Rijksmuseum: II

Rudolph, do you remember how we met?
I answered your ad and we arranged
to meet in the Rijksmuseum. Shh
I know exactly what you thought
No, let me finish – then I'll come to bed

"I'm a military man. Art
is not worth wasting time over
here's three acres of
painting and carving by men
without the sense to take what's offered

Give an artist some fruit and wine
or a naked courtesan on a couch
and he'll start fiddling with shade and texture
meanwhile any man with common sense
will have eaten the fruit, gulped the wine
laid the woman, and not wasted canvas
perfectly good for patching tents

Take this Rembrandt: there's hardly
enough light to show us what he was missing
while he painted away

But you, walking towards me
now there's lines for the taking, the way
your long legs lead to two good handfuls of ass
a pretty little waist and long smooth arms
dark hair, full lips and fatal eyes
even an artist might notice
(he'd knock over the easel

on the way to the couch)
All those painters aiming at Eve should see you
your walk that says Paradise is still here
I'll open those gates, girl, so your beauty
knocks the figures off their plinths
Truth, Justice, Honour, Virtue shattering
under the attack of honest lust
I'll describe the Tropics
and the dangers of my work
while I maneuver you onto that couch
we'll turn art back into life
or your hips are lying to me
and I know how to read hips"

How's that, Rudy? Wake up, you drunk
your little wife dramatized your inmost thoughts
and you missed it. All right, I'm coming to bed

My Son as a New Island

No one knows all the islands of
the Java Sea. In this region
geography is no solid science
the earth's blood boils, a raw cone
pushes through steaming ocean
waves unfurl like eyelids after a long sleep

New island
soon vines snake and fasten, orchids bloom
trees root to nothing known
birds discuss eventualities

No one walks this shore
meeting the sea like a torn hem
no map has squared it with parallels
or announced a new name
to long for

How soon the cycle reverses
sea's womb reopens
rock swims into the vanishing point
vines dive through watery declensions
of green. Astounded fish watch
an orchid drift past

And the unknown island is one more
wreck in the ocean's lap, one word
murmured
for the sake of forgetting

Fist of No

Meet the happy couple
domestic and useful

I am slender, sharp and bright
and slammed into the floor
by this hammer of a husband

His fist's a stuck telegraph key
that pounds out the same word
over and over NO

Meinher Hammer likes things simple
A nail goes in straight or wrong. Sober or drunk
obey him or disobey

Attack or retreat, sex/sleep
attention or at ease. All my choices knocked down to his
while the gamelan orchestra
on the jasmine breeze plays the harmony
of a hundred other possibilities

To him I am a jungle warp of curves
he must flatten into a cenotaph
No to what my dreams suggest
No to the beauty other men see
No to anything but the weight of his will

Husband, beware. The slender nail
sings long after it is hit
pierces the floor and is gone
Without me you're an iron head
that has lost the only word it knows

Typhoid Fever

Typhoid takes me
steam in the brain
lose touch with life
as I know it
explore elsewhere: reconnaissance
know it over or not at all
under the white sun of spring
sap boils out of treetops
forms a phantom tree

lose control
over me: mother wife invalid
I'm in-valid will never be
any sane agony
the same again

it hurts to change
knots of thunder in my joints
blood boils like stagnant water
when something rots underneath

shivers and stings and mal de mer
and mother's tears
for babies Pik and Jan Fluit

one's gone, poisoned for sins
of the elders, sick old story
the warm climes unhealthy
but soft (here under the pith helmet
dyked by gun and culture and royal decree)
stern cold Dutch safe

I'm a Frisian with fever
don't resemble
any other
I must be a foundling
recessive gene they say
can't disguise the Jewish blood in me
can't hide the Javanese in me

she's not one of us
I'm not one of you
fairy child gone, boiled away
brain soup, cauliflower, white sun
who am I in the great solvent
of sickness
fever child watching ballerinas dance
first position green on black
wallpaper, fevered swim
through sheets of sloughed-off skin
in monsoon
no names here
you're a sick woman
I'm a sick woman, yes

don't drink don't breathe
speak only to natives
as if they were servants

my child, my son
black vomit over his face
"Mama, help me, help"
cure something the father did
(fucked/ killed/ ordered
soldier business)

my son, gone, monsoon
rain washing everything off
the thatched roof, the palms
hand is destiny, mudras, mantras
the hand knows what to say
mine is hot
lines writhe snakily

changing courses in mid-dream
new fevers of form, malcontent
sucking my force into their fog roots
brain on a string pegged to body
that fever strums storms, cloud

I'm cold, shower of sweat
something's prowling through tendrils and vine
a shadow weaving moiré patterns

an idea loose from the zoo of form
tiger / Maya / all is void
hunting me, meaning, moans
come awake breaking through skin of dream
and my husband's voice like a grater
"Five guilders a day for the milk for her
five guilders a day"

no, I'm not worth it
pour the milk in
fat and chalk on my tongue
and it becomes fever cloud
blood on the horns of moon
fall back and let fever steam my brain
barely attached

stem to an out-of-whack watch
counting how long sick takes to strike
snakes crawling
up my wrist
to wave their rattles for baby
who'll drop into sweet sleep
bailing out fragile craft of my being
with a broken glass
in it the fever settles

from ashes I arise
at last I know who I'm
not

Debut at the Musée Guimet, Paris

My dance is a sacred poem in which each movement is a word and whose every word is underlined by music. Mata Hari to her audience, after the performance that launched her career.

Golden collar around my throat, pearls on my tawny arms
and legs
I stand in a fog of incense, incantation from
sitar and tabla
faces stuffed with Parisian art and money goggling at me

I dance for the statue facing me, Shiva
in his aspect of King of Dancers
his right foot crushing the dwarf of ignorance, left upraised
perfect balance with four arms above, face calm
halo of flame and emanations
scrolling from his ears

The truth of dance animates me
I take my past, my grief, my marriage
my failure as wife, artist's model, circus rider
my arrival in the City of Light
half a franc and a revolver in my purse
nothing to trade but my body and wits

I crush all beneath my feet, crush and re-create myself
strip the flesh and long dark hair
of Margaretha Gertruuida Zelle MacLeod
away from my bones
stamp her bones to dust and sweep it away
with my hands
now birds, now flames, now invitations to sexual frenzy

The Parisians have never seen anything like this
They know someone is dying, someone being seduced
but aren't sure who

This drama is older than Paris
whose centuries are one posture in Shiva's dance
whose Opera and sieges and guillotines
are symptoms of his music and fire
scouring human dirt from the planet
until the metal at the centre shines through

I offer my life through my body
to my lord of creation destruction
and bear a new woman through jeweled loins

Afterward I tell the crowd Shiva's story in French
then in English, German, Dutch, Javanese
They know to join my dance is to forget themselves
My final gesture seduces each one of them
into the abyss of mystery

Each feels a shiver that starts at the genitals
and runs straight up the spine
sparking the urge to say

Fuck the family, fuck the past, civilization,
my tiresome self
Junk the lot and start anew
Care to dance

Salomé

In 1911, after a long pursuit of the role, Mata Hari danced the part of Salomé at the Palazzo Barberini. Richard Strauss's opera was inspired by Oscar Wilde's writing, and was considered the height of decadence.

What *Carmen* only hints at, this opera shrieks
Women murder as well as they conceive
using all the power of mistress
mother, harpy

Kali, consort of Shiva, incarnates seduction
yet human skulls form her necklace
She dances on the corpse heap of men she's killed
before she consumes them

The praying mantis eats her mate
as dessert during copulation
She who gives life takes it back
This opera states a truth
that convention denies
I was born to dance this role
my mastery of men a rehearsal

Herod wants her body, slowly revealed
Salomé the head of that prophet
so inflated with future holiness
that it floated away from her beauty
towards God

Offered anything she wants
all she will reply is "the head of Iokannon"

Since then only virgins can be holy
Christians mortify their flesh, fast
call sex a ruse of Satan
When I dance Salomé I'll take their heads off
while the music cracks and thumps
like a soul forced back into flesh

My body the revelation, the fruit, the truth
my arms become, my thighs crack bones
eyes the windows of an ancient temple
tinting a sacrifice with honeyed light
I strip off the veils until my body gleams through
the king groans, comes on his throne
and the prophet's head shoots from his body
because he finally remembers what a woman is
the chalice of life, death, the newly born

I ravish the audience and withdraw
they applaud, cannot even look at each other

I have made sex holy
my body ringing doom like a gong
a sound they'll only hear again
when someone dances them away for good

Figurehead Dream

A buxom wooden woman painted in bright polychrome
I cut the waves at a good clip
as wind flutes through my chiseled hair
water foams over my polished waist
"She's got a bone in her teeth," old sailors said
watching a clipper split the waves like this

Ships are "she" because their figureheads
breast the water and men try to make them
obey with ropes knots and wise old saws
I'm a figurehead who's quit her ship
My lips fix a grin
Men don't want these complexities

Bone in my teeth
figure of speech caught in my head
tongue sealed by salt wind

Grey destroyers hunt me
their massive bows curled like absolute physics
fade into mist as they taper behind
They arc and skid on the sea
trying to split my wood with metal
pass through each other like ghosts

I aim my painted smile at the future
My wake's a wedge of bubbling surf
that the ships bisect and bury
They close on me as the red sun
rises and paints the ocean with fire

I catch and torch into an icon
The destroyers dull to fillets of spent force
Steaming water streams behind me
like a bridal veil
I ascend the column of my burning
Figurehead to the sky

Madrid Tango

Palace Hotel, Madrid, New Year's Eve, 1916

The tango is perfect seduction
a warm breeze from the shores of Argentina
the perfect dance for all the double agents here
we glide across the floor in pairs
our feet moving smoothly as a snake's ribs
I hardly know who holds my hand
he is slender and proud
and does not know all that I am
in the addiction of tango we drop our masks

I am not unproductive agent H21
the ex-performer or aging charmer
I am pure feminine essence
as silken as my gown
and he is only a man
the music's magnet forms our elements
into straight lines that cross the floor
reverse, fall back in two/four time

this dance is brandy in our veins
flamenco slowed by South American sun

we pass the blonde French woman
who often whispers to my chambermaid
held by Prince Ratibor, the new German ambassador
there is the little man who shadowed me
behind potted palms in the Paris Hotel
his suspicions forgotten as he stares
into a Portuguese agent's eyes

any woman could become a spy
she already knows the first rule
never show the enemy what you really want
wear the mask he finds most pleasing

I have been dancer, courtesan, spy
like Shiva I destroy as my quick feet create
tonight I'm no one but a woman
who never let the past direct her steps

and you, holding me, are any man
from a dozen nations – allied, neutral, pro-German
what you want from me
is not information, gratification or applause
but a body that knows you'll turn
before you do
a back that sings violin to your hand
an elegant arm that stretches as far as yours
so we turn and strut and lean

at midnight all kiss, and champagne corks
salute the artillery a few hundred miles away
Noisemakers blow out like tongues of the dead
a new year for this tired war

I've had enough of suspecting
and being suspected in turn
the cure for my malaise is more tango
tango across the curling ribbons of
squashed funny hats and broken glasses

I'll trade any secret for one more dance
and you'll destroy your career

for me aging and ageless
beautiful and sad, sore feet, a hangover
but my eyes still reflect the dawn

although morning dispels the tango like fog
part of me dances still
among the snoring spies and empty bottles
masks and mirrors of the Palace Hotel
tangoing with a shadow that suggests
all the men who ever wanted me

Trial by Tongues

Military Tribunal, Paris, July, 1917

As for myself, I have been sincere. My life and my self-interest are the guarantee of that. Today, around me, everything is collapsing, everyone turns his back, even he for whom I would have gone through fire. Never would I have believed in so much human cowardice. Well, so be it. I am alone. I will defend myself and if I must fall it will be with a smile of profound contempt.

Mata Hari,
in a letter written a month before her trial

We all know what's going to happen here
why bother going through these formalities
The jurors are to answer yes or no
to whether I betrayed France in eight different ways
one yes is excuse enough
for a firing squad to perform its little routine

The prosecution weaves French inflections
into a shimmering web. As in espionage
language must be opaque
nothing meaning what it says
much like modern poetry
where a speeding car means woman
a woman who stands for time

The Germans sent a telegram in code
they knew the French could break
in it was the code for me
Spectators appreciate my fine French
my lucidity, my verve but the jury's ears

open only for the accent of French honour
bruised and skinned in this unwinnable war

It must be my fault, I am here, notorious
the government needs good press
my lovers and patrons will not speak to this court
my own words are turned against me
they try to prove my contraceptive cream
is a clever disguise for secret ink

Verbs strip me, adjectives lash and cut
hot nouns brand my prison-faded skin
codes and phrases tighten around my neck

I who speak five languages, love poetry
played Salomé, whose hips could take off
a prophet's head

Although I defend myself well, my old fool
of a lawyer stutters and splutters, archaic footnotes
tack his tongue to his palate

Language is how we handle the world
yet its wrapping conceals reality
the art of Maya
is to name, call out, denounce

I hear the feet of the dancer whose steps destroy
even in this French military court
where the prosecution's logical cannon besiege me
in the cadences and rhetorical flourishes
fired beneath French mustaches

My work for the Germans
killed 50,000 Allied soldiers, they say
let us then apportion the blame
10,000 corpses for each melancholy dark eye
whole regiments for each shapely knee
a division swept aside by my elegant arms
(the most beautiful in the world, an admirer said)
but all the rest rot in a trench
dug and mined by my lying tongue
that said one thing
the prosecution shows, clearly meaning another

I was a double agent, double meaning
une agente horizontale, the bed my campaign field
back in my prison cell I was in good company
two decades ago Madame Steinhel stayed here
whose tongue so delighted the President of France
his heart stopped as he clutched her curly head
to his loins. He died happier
than this grim jury will ever be

but my wind wanders
They prepare the verdict, sentence
"I must die" the message concealed
under this interminable code of a trial

Incandescence

The sun on the mountains turned
to storm and what went
through us could have been anything
in its instant
rock turned to cloud
the Greek alphabet in newness

but the lightning took
a tree instead of us
and we escaped, scared normal humans
before a second stroke made us
saints and cinders

does any lightning bring me
back on your line
the way it snaps stills for me
of you on the rock that day

Ghost

An alteration of the air at the Villa Rémy
shadows dappling a brown horse seem
to rise and turn into a woman riding

the robe of wind whirls around a node where
dusty
leaves spin a garment for the forest mistress
of shadowed trails and pools of light
a garment of loss, dancing around no body

when the wine is gone a different bouquet remains
air taking on lightness
such is my ghost: the world, mother of all
cannot stand to lose everything of her children
so keeps our most volatile parts
to flavour the wind
after the wine is drunk, bottle smashed

in the sad dark of the garage where the Daimlers
and Peugeots purred for my guests
the signal of my eyes still flashes

on the steps where I posed, a statue of desire
carved by the gazes of wealthy men
my absence forms a longing the visitor cannot place

these forms hold as much truth as the other
tales about my execution

that at "Fire!" I threw off my coat

my nakedness dazzled the twelve Zouaves so much
they shot two larks and ten paths of air
and I escaped
to live out my old age
or it was a publicity ploy
morale-building for a war-tired public
blanks in the guns and after the performance
champagne and kisses as usual in a limousine
(unlikely because so few have the courage
to enter a fairy tale)

I prefer this: I spun on my dancer's soles
like a dervish, boring down into
the earth as rifles spat above
I swam through earth's boiling heart and
came up through a Java volcano where
worshipped by natives fanning me with palm fronds
I advise young girls on
how to love and not lose
or I am Hari's comet crossing the skies
whenever a great man is brought down by lust

we need ghosts because facts are so brutal, dull
I was shot though the heart, my face blown off
with a forty-five caliber coup de grâce
and the body that Europe once worshipped
carted off to medical students for dissection

that is only the body's truth
the spirit that made me dance
rides that horse though shifting shadows
in a forest afternoon forever

The Boulder

Near Rivière-du-Loup
above the sweeping St. Lawrence
a granite heart
taller than a man
interrupts a seigneural field
otherwise perfectly plowed

Rock maintained its place since the first settler
switched his ox around it and swore
one day he'd dig that boulder out

but over the years
the river below filling and flowing with the tide
that jog in plowing became part of the dance
farmer and seasons performed with the land
the earth below his clogs mud
then awash in wheat, then frozen
the boulder unchanging
touchstone, always winter in heart

The farmer's son swore too
first at the boulder
then that it would go
as did his son's son and grandson
each came to respect it
could not afford the void
yanking it would make in his life

the boulder withstood them all
as it now withstands my eyes

I swear this poem will move it
for my lines cut straight
(yet the boulder sits)

Industrial Arts Dream

The industrial artist chartered a copter
to drop the critics and corporate patrons
at the bottom of the gravel pit
that a bemused absentee-landlord
holding company let him use
for what he said would be *definitive* on
how technology changes landscape

The audience surveyed the work
as the artist waved from the chopper
now perched on the quarry's rim
lava flowed towards their feet
down one side a torrent of electrical cable
wrapped in black
exposed copper filaments like nerves
beside it, some blue chemical declined in slow waves
that popped in iridescent bubbles

Across the pit, constructing a balancing diagonal mass
a surf of white foam descended
the quarry's side could be seen only
between a mobile of PCB-daubed transformer parts
and the trellis of used bridge struts dipped in crude
how pleasing to note the umber simplicity of earth
not only as a reminder of the ground
against which all art figures
but also for its suggestion of an avenue of escape

As one, pundits and patrons moved towards the path
masking worry in discourse of earthworks, trash art

driving a stake through the heart of modernism
above them some diesel machine
uttered a ribbon of glowing slag
to cover the last stripe of earth
and complete the installation

Baffled, the audience stood and turned
art at last bigger than they were
yet somehow they completed it
their tiny cries adding that note of angst
that kept the piece from descending to one more gloss
on the well-worn theme of our rape of the earth

Edville

Written while living two blocks away from Honest Ed's, the "world's biggest discount store"

Circus lights shout Honest Ed
over and over, three stories high
and two blocks long, a legend built of tiny bulbs
that burn all night in buy-buy-binary code
Ed, in his honesty, owns
the block and more. He bought it by selling
for less more than anyone else. And he never
sold out to modesty. Every word ever written
about him is displayed in the windows to prove
the world turns to Ed
to see just how cheap a man can be
turns into Ed, or fails

Take the Edsel. Ford should have asked Ed
before launching it. He would have made the car
a hit, his face set into the grille's
halo of chrome. Take the moon
The Yanks got there without Idea One
what to do with it. Ed, in his space suit
and tie, writ large with funny sayings and
bargain boasts, would have zoned it for Sunday openings
and sold the dark side to insomniacs
the craters to park flying saucers
the moon dust to scour the pots of the poor
always willing to line up
for a deal from Ed. Because
there's no place like this place anyplace
Now the shadow of the CN Tower

points like an hour hand
from Ed's restaurants to his store
and a flotilla of security guards, chestnut sellers
and buyers of busts of the Pope
sets out in the rolling wake
of his Edship
the Lord Mayor of Edville
the megaphone of himself

Renovating Hell

Even Hell must keep up
When the soul still knew its way
physical torture sufficed
but levers, racks and furnaces broke down
eternal punishment left no maintenance time
Dante's demons tired after centuries
of the stink of sinners in their own shit
Beelzebub for his part
suffered from the symphony flies
always wove around him
he began to take calls from
the cell phones of the damned
felt compassion for clients
backstroking through the brimstone

Now the lost soul finds bleak greeting rooms
burning with cool, fluorescent light
Hades and purgatory merged to cut costs
Muzak plays songs the soul once loved
needled by oversweet strings

You always need one more
identity card or number and at every obstacle
transistorized greeting cards chirp
meaningless pledges of encouragement
You will never get well, be processed
leave this place. Or even learn
what you wait for

Mephistopheles lounges
outside the control room where
the automated tapes loop
that echo down the halls
outside, in the sunlight
the flies tumble and sing
they too were fired by
Hell's modernization plan

The Child Murderer

The child murderer buys a
newspaper to see his latest work reviewed
the coins he paid for the paper
radiate the warmth of his strong hand
as they lie in the register
his new shoes creak slightly
like a sign swinging in the wind

He is as careful with all details
the gloves, the anonymous rope, the plastic bag
as he is with his clothes
He walks down the street with
a secret delight normal things magnify
dog tethered to a parking meter
the ferns outside the florist's
"Maybe" he thinks "I'll send a card
Sympathy from a Friend"
He, only he, can get away with it
To charm then chill
without contradiction
a man among men
he skims the other news on a park bench
adjusts the flower in his lapel
sparrows fly from crumbs at his feet
he smiles at a child, and stands

Parliament St. Tableau

A man is parked
on his back by the curb
in a suit torn and grey
arms legs weakly waving
like a rolled-over beetle
One side of his face
raw red meat. The blood
draws eyes, wino hurt

Two cops vertical pillars
who ignore normally his pain
look down, blue arms folded
at his hands offering gestures
as if explaining himself

Xmas Pageant, 1961

At thirteen, I was the United Church's Joseph
my Mary a girl from College Avenue
so virginal that a blush
was new, disturbed her
our babe a doll with oversized rubber head
smelled like Eaton's
three wise men, resplendent in striped
bathrobes, towel turbans and
itchy cotton beards
brought gift-wrapped boxes of emptiness
frankincense was hard to find in Guelph
myrrh too bitter for Ontario

I thought Mary and I should at least
have a crush on each other
in Christmas spirit, when miracles
births, warm animals and new stars
crowding the manger seemed sexy
At thirteen, nearly everything did
but she was as impossible to talk to
as a Japanese schoolgirl
Only in the dumb show of the pageant
could we touch, moist hands rehearsing
first step of high school courtship

I had spent the Christmas before in Iraq
the hills bleached and biblical
still bore sheep shepherds wearing real robes
goat songs fluted off the rocks
miracles were so long ago

they had worn to tracings on sun-blasted brick
December was heat and sandstorms
expensive stale goodies from the British import store
and chips and lemonade around the swimming pool
of the equally-British Alwiyah club

Back in Guelph I learned to step between worlds
It was no stranger to play Joseph
with my white face and cracking voice
framed by snow sifting along the windows
than for Mary with another exquisite blush
to produce from my fertile imagining
a babe quiet and perfect enough

to bring teen-aged wise men
with boxes of empty promise

Dead Skunk on the Don Valley Parkway

You smell, now, no worse
than the trucks rolling
on and around your blot of fur

Lanes leaf and merge everywhere
yet you made your way here, halfway
across, before something your bouquet

Couldn't stop cancelled you
you came, perhaps, to dance
among the white dashes and streaks

That define this black roadway
like hard-edge skunk art gone mad
Maybe you had the time wrong

A century ago, between wolf, fox and
hawk, you moved calmly here, your power held
under your tail's exclamation mark

Then, no one charged you at 100 per
In skunk time you made sense
Here, now, you catch only my eye

and I must drive on. But you cling
to me still, like the sweet inside your stink
your midnight dance's grace

Leaving the Cape

Cape Traverse, PEI

Leaving the Cape
means pulling yourself out of a jigsaw
you were surprised you fit

Tiger lilies burning up the rain
silver spider webs linking them
herons musing in the stream that fills
and empties, empties and fills
as shore bares and hides
its rippled sweep

In honour of your departure
a garland of kelp
garnished with mauve Irish moss
and set with immaculate shells spent
by the prodigal sea

So load the car, lock the door
take a last lungful of air
nourishing as broth
then leave again
this living place that will stay
for you in closets and Kodachromes
but this is only the human side
tides and clouds fill back in
this small gap in the puzzle
your leaving means

Ode to the TD Bank

On asking for my first loan

I have lived at the same address so long
that mail is slid through my mouth
and strangers grasp my hand to open
the door. Although I remain unmarried
all women work for me and offer up
their assets. The stars of the sky
I keep as jewels in my eye's vault
I sleep in stocks and drink nothing
but bonded

In fact limestone banks
chase me along the street trailing tapes
and begging for my magic valve kiss
to release the pressure of their
respectability. Most of all
I ask for money because I do not
even remotely need it, but only intend
to honour that minor art form
the won loan
which sustains all Bay Street

For Erinann

Small and new, you turn into me
as if you'd crawl inside where nothing hurts
If I could open this man's body
I'd tuck you under my ribs
and warm you in the infra of my heart

You whimper, awake, then instantly dream
and forget the sharp things cold lights and
hurts the world out here holds

Forget the isolette that held you
a clear oven for your little loaf
On your smile you slide back
to where you were always held
and cushioned and fed
put your hands by your face again
the pose that made your birth take so long.

Maybe if you'd held them that way forever
you'd still be riding the best ship there is
instead of this cold train
of emergency, test and therapy
Crawl into me, small girl
I'm holding my ribs up like an umbrella

Exorcism

I

Whenever I touch too deeply
it brings back the Latin lover from long ago
his ghost's hand's stuck so deep in your heart
that he flips it away like a pizza
any time I get too close

II

Worse, he doesn't even know he's haunting us
his bodily form's balding in the Beaches
going for boardwalks with his meal ticket
who you're glad to hear is heavy
around the thighs. Visitations from the living
are more difficult to clear

III

Unreal though he is, his shadow
shrinks me again. Can I ever love you
as much as he hurt you? A difficult equation
our brains start weighing while damnit
he's back in our bed again
dividing us like an equal sign

IV

Here's what we'll do, love: exorcise him
he wanted to be a writer, so
I'll pen him in this pentacle of words
while you light three candles with your tears
incant his name over and over
until it's as void as any national brand's

V

And when the glaze slides over his face
freezing him home, in front of the tube
we'll trap him in a slot of dead time
a car chase cut off, bullet suspended
in air like a hypnotized bee
and though there'll always be that handprint
on your heart, our bed will hold only us
no ghosts. A new start

Back to You

On my fingers your scent
weaves a line through day
back to you
even the business letters I type
breathe a petaled smell
like perfume on the shoulder
of a three-piece suit

What I learn of you starts
to thread parts of the world together
"Your tiny hands are frozen" the aria
your grandfather, 90, still sang to you
and I find it again in the book I read
after leaving you that day

My sweat lines your sheets
and now you find companion bed
colder and quieter when
I'm not in it
I know when you feel my absence
like I've known few things
It's holding a rock in my hand long
enough that it's warm as blood
Then I know as much as you can about
rock, about another

Variations on a Theme by Erik Satie

Delicately placed
spaces in between the notes
state the other melody
the one not heard

Who says we only tune in
one channel at a time?

You do, silently
you turn away, leave
break it off

Between each gesture
the ghost of you, happy to see me
face lit up by the lamp of me
clothes flying off like leaves
from the lovely tree
underneath

In your stillness
I hear that other you singing
why, o why, o why
not?
Delicately placing me
in you
between the notes and
the nots

I'm in Love with my Hoover

Today I declared my love at last
to my Hoover: plugged her in
lay down beside her on the rug
touched her power switch with my tongue
and let myself go in the sweet rush
of in-drawing air

I love the way she empties
the dust-filled corners of my life
She vanishes the rejection slips
failed poems, duplicate bills
that fill my mail. I always take her now
when the doorbell rings
A pimply boy selling chocolate bars
to benefit his school: I Hoovered him up
Another salesman, this time for a version
of the word of the Lord. Hoovered him too
My whole family – Hoovered! No more long
distance calls, Christmas gifts, guilt
I Hoovered off my mustache, then my whole face
Sweet vacuum of anonymity
Is she my real mother? I'll only know
when I Hoover the rest of me
into the busy peace at the center
of her cyclone song

Stroke/Oblique

For my mother

An errant line stopped its flow
to your left brain
like an oblique/ canceling a name
a cerebral-vascular accident
caused by a fragment of arterial plaque
loose in the sanguine tide
that ebbs and whispers along the organ pipes
and flourishes of the body

now in half your brain nothing moves
but snow, falling in endless hush

Seeing you in the hospital at 2:30 a.m.
I thought you might die
but day by day you put more back together
than anyone thought you could
first you know your children's faces
but not our names
and then with your manners as proper as ever
delicately hold the spoon upside down
try to balance bland hospital morsels on it
when handed your toothpaste you gravely
consult the mirror and spread
Crest neatly round your lips
At seventy-three you relearn the simple things of life
while in the left half of your brain
nothing but snow sliding down

Asked to write your name you carefully letter
"QUART"
you who took on the *Globe*'s Friday cross-word
every week
"gyre" and "owlet" (Hamlet's night bird?) familiar
as the irises in your garden
which you still admire but can't identify

Those nights we sat by the fire around a card table
and played Scrabble where words count triple
now few words come out the way you will
although you know what you want to say
snow slips between the syllables
and your intelligence can't
find the way out
from your eyes the same smart little girl
whose family couldn't understand
looks out to see if I comprehend
mirrored in my eyes you see snow
obliques your meaning

At first you are reduced to the elements
of a nod, a smile, a hand's assent
you regain language like an earthquake survivor
rebuilding her house, stone by stone

One image of you
my brain will hold until it stills
you doze in a chair near the cabin
shaded from late August sun

the same place your dying daughter sat ten years ago
and the loss and grief leave your face
revealing its strength and gentleness
comfortable in your bones, among the caroling birds
you once knew by name
you sit safe in a word
bigger than any I know

Canadian Love Song

Instructions: read out loud either
A) nude in a forest during the summer or
B) while a friend hums as high as possible and
occasionally slaps your body.

I have an itch
which is you
calamine pink
mosquito blue

Floating I smell
your tender skin
the blood you bubble
to draw me in

I've got an itch
that wants your bite
in humming sun
in hatching night

Your touch sings
"Sting me awake
Scratch away these
weeks without wings"

In tent, in bag
portaging canoe
mosquito pink
calamine blue

The Perceivability of Poetry

"The Native Hollander wears wooden shoes."
"Nebraska has no seacoast."
"The daisy is a common wildflower."
As these syllables, words and sentences come in over the telephones, stand-ins for millions of Bell System subscribers rate them for clarity of reception.

Bell Tel ad in 1959 *Scientific American*

True, few will listen when poetry calls
they think they've got the wrong line
a harangue in some exotic tongue
satellite call from Mars
subscription offer to eternity

but I'm here to tell you
Nebraska has no sequels
the daisy has come in wildfire
Nate, in colander wares, wouldn't choose
and this news has the clarity of any you receive
poetry's in the curve from mouth to ear
even as we talk, we agitate carbon grains
that squeeze our words into a spiral cord
and boil them out the other end
you still say poetry isn't clear
Well, the word is a wildly common weed
but I seek no hose nor will Ned ask her
and the days you see are wood
shooting onto a seacoast

what has more clarity than a daisy?
And yet I mean by daisy: time, change
pollen on the flying legs of bees
the sun surrounded by our white faces

the shaded meaning of any word
the petals that burst from the ear
when I sing

now tell me what you heard in what I said
and I'll let you go

The White Page

In memory of bp nichol

Facing the white page
its feature: featurelessness
Make the first mark, start, invoke a chain
that pulls down the curtain on the other chains
The page, white
Arctic expanse, space gone crazy. Go
crazy, pee your name
in drifting loops across the page
calligraph it with a brush dipped in gas
sign it with a match. The burning page
frozen

Erase. Delete. Recover
the page still white. White always. Waiting
nose to the page, you feel distant movement
molecules chanting along the lines, rhythm
a tiny black dot in the white distance
all words condensed into one whole
dot growing, racing at you
Doppler effect of sidebands, parallel text
sliding tones pulled along in the slipstream
the whole page, black, bursting around you
roar in your ears of many languages, multiple
lines. Black shreds of punctuation eclipse, fall away

The page white again, but now a negative
from memory you begin to fill the page, alter it
telling the page, lining its altar with
your symbols finally aligned

the cup, the cloth, speaking lips
the blood-red wine alters the memory
you were never Catholic
is the page now someone else's? Strike out. Crumple
a match to it. Reflecting: this white page
writing as the shadow, adumbration, not too much light
on the subject. Leave room for language
to uncoil in the shade
Page, bring me my helmet and sword
Is it false to take meaning from the sound
aren't all things signs
slaying the page with a single stroke
writer's dream on white sheets of night
coming back to dance on the page
next morning. Feet brush by like vowels
along the lip of the page. Still white
the heart of the page. Untouched, unlined
acquiescent, questioning. Mute, demanding
state that mind never achieves
it's so lined with words with music
hunger for the white page

William Tell's Son Speaks

I do wish Dad
would give up on this
but he stands there still, too far away
one eye pulled into a paternal squint
sighting along that damned shaft
while I wait, absurd, still life
with an apple in my hair

At this point in my storybooks
someone gallops to the rescue
maybe the Lone Ranger
riding the wave of his overture
to point out with his Colt Forty-five
how my father might reconsider
this practice of targeting me
but no hooves arrive

"Have faith," Father tells me
"I never miss"
"Miss once, and I'll be never"
I mutter, but he doesn't hear
one ear tuned to his Swiss watchmaker God
the other to the wavering wind

So I'm Isaac and he's willing to bet me
on one more test of his belief
or he's Isaac Newton, set to kill
the apple of gravity with the arrow
of his thought. Me, I'm just a body at rest

What does he need me for
He could skewer this fruit on a fence post
with just as fine a shot. A post that would also
look better wearing a miss
than my smooth boy's brow would
but it's too late to tell him anything
his fingers are releasing the string
while his lips hiss: "This is for you
son!"

The World Screened

The world through your window
is screened into rows of tiny cubes

that means we can remake
the world by shifting them

a pure pane of sky shines
from the pine's arthritic roots

the library is strewn along the walk
which itself winds over

branches, bedrooms. Shadows of things start
elsewhere and cross where they might be cloud

the pedestrian's two left eyes
regard the sun strolling on her leash

as they move cube by cube over the clear blue lawn
her heart is (not is like) a bird

Note My Father Wrote Me Sixteen Years Ago

This is the first time
I have appeared in a poem

        Your disappearances short (temper & work)
        Long (losing interest in this family)

I have taken trouble, now
to conceal my identity

        Then you must have known
        finally, who you were

I have dyed my hair green. I
am getting to the count-down stage

        Tanks full, silver nose
        aimed at the silent stars

Just gave my scientific books to the
local university. Came in with zero

        Snapshot: you at six, short pants, holding up
        tray of baby chicks: small, warm zeros

Plan to leave the stage
at that level, too

        You take with you
        what you've left behind

Jack   John

Progress

When I was small, my parents
were immaculate edifices
Mom with her superstructure of intricate dark hair
Dad's pipe a smokestack
towering over me so
hugely and maybe they had everything
I needed, on one floor or another

Now that I am larger and
look down on both of them
seeing their imperfections
with the zoom lens of an angel
I wonder how they could betray me
be so human

The Banquet

Grey and shy, the head table
guest has never been invited
to a banquet before, yet
guests arrive on stylish wings
clad in dazzling gold and black, always in fashion
Plumper business buzzers too
with cummerbunds of iridescent blue-green
all are ready to feast

Mr. Mouse, head taken clean away
by a cat's offhand swipe
flashes vivid hues under mousy drab
standard response is "gruesome"
but in the shadow of my paused foot
a banquet is underway

Why the Branch Came Down

The stress of high winds
one cyclist said, or the weight
of fall morning dew

Dragonfly Day

Full summer expands
into the day when in lake air
all small dragonflies must mate
orange-head male's tail tucked
just behind yellow-head female's thorax

Each couple, courting to copulate
darts tandem inches over the lake
that my canoe cuts wake through
light suspends pollen and eggs
in the water that instills us all

A rare single insect
frantically tries to couple with
floating twigs, other males. Whatever
it must be done today
Dragonflies ready the eggs
in which their future flies

Remember you astride me in the dunes
behind the beach, our only foreplay talk
wet swimsuits pulled aside
you fly over me
with full July sun in my eyes
then transparent wings appear and
sew onto our backs
as tourists gawk and cameras wink
lift-off at last

Report of the Task Force to Eliminate the Lyric Reflex

Since that O! impulse
produced regrettable flourishes
of metaphor and emotional meanderings
it is now thoroughly discredited
by guaranteed theory

I can report while
sitting in the background with the grey cat
both of us saying nothing
we observed rude sparrows and
subtle breezes running waves through the hedge
as tired symptoms of reality-apprehension
hardly worth recording
To further increase the effect
I drew somber clouds over the clichéd sunlight
and erased that rain-drunk snail
inscribing silver calligraphy
across the pitted walk

The world is now blank. No
it doesn't matter how you feel
about this. The work proceeds

Valentine's Day

The onflowing current is time
taking us from source to ocean
slowly its turbulence makes
us half spin
While young, we look only
ahead to cities of adult privilege
and imagine the freedoms
we will inhabit there
After some aging
we look back and wonder
how we have flowed from that
young self who still saw hope

But we can also turn within ourselves
displacing for a moment the pain and weight
our voyage has found and say "I start here
This is me, new." This you do

Time Slip

Newspaper article, December, 1999: Quantum physicists argue that linear clock time is an illusion, and that "time slip" (an outbreak of a past reality in the present) is possible, even probable.

the moment turns: a tumbler
like you, rolling a car over again
about to break a power pole, shut off the neighborhood
wondering in that elastic instant that suspends lives
whether you will survive this crash, too
opaque future walls up vision
the big-handed past insists you
and your choices and your family drove
you again to this moment of suspension

(time/slip)
anxious to see anything that looks land
I tumble down from the crow's nest
no albatrosses around and as my bare feet spin
in North Atlantic gusts I can't decide whether
I'd rather die on the splintered deck
simulacrum of land or in
the glacial sea I never learned to swim

(time/slip)
Should we sign the death warrant?
Bother to write a suicide note?
Keep on producing poems hardly anyone'll hear
when the sun had only 4.5 billions years
of hydrogen left to fuse into helium
and collapsed laughing as the
universe in sympathy retracted

into the unimaginable mother point
in which all lines lie coiled

(time/slip)
"But I was so much older then
I'm younger than that now"
When they begin the beguin-
ning, what will be may be
Should auld acquaintance
be sweet futurity
Daisy, Daisy, give me your onset
do, for the days of for-sure past
are no longer foregone
do change the channel
the channel changes you

(time/slip)
consider the sneeze
"God bless you"
signals the Black Death
followed by rings around the rosy
buboes, and extinction
Farewell, my village. Let us eat moldy rye bread
so we can hallucinate angels descending
we are born to die
to write, sing is to rebel
against this terrible interminable
sentence. Seize: life as a sneeze
that blesses itself
after the long silence of suspense
before the next long silence ends

For doth not Sun dance

attendance upon the stalwart Earth
as it must, and is not Man
one scant rung below the Angels
and must not all Living Things
have a stable Abode

(time/slip)
No. All is relative
My stillness makes you move
"I" is just a formula for
me as perceived from your position and velocity
tiring of this site
on the Möbius striptease of space
shredding its time wear
I approach the speed of light
thus slowing time and making infinite
my mass. Holy Heavy. Like Jenny Craig run backwards
at high speed. Or the highwayman come
riding up to the old In door
while the highway was Out
riding away from him

(time/slip)
Your car turns, falls
you stare down into blue sky

(time/slip)
Strike the tambour, bodhran
dai taiko! Strum
the sitar, guitar, zither, al oud, that lute
dance, feet that pace off space,
behold they keep time
penned and pining. We cannot wait

to begin the begui-
ling dance, or for steps
to end, for joy of the dance
is the unanticipated but apt final move
floor seguing up to meet Astaire's feet
just as he comes down the wall

(time/slip)
how we laugh
blue with woad
lying under the sacred oak
ripping Druid truth
because we're also sipping fine tea and wearing silk
about to meet a real Princess
and we're collaborating
on a courtly masque that will lampoon
the lice under lace and perfume

(time/slip)
while we're trying to make this thin earth
and northern sun pronounce together just one word
po-ta-to just say it, damn it
and we will eat the word
to save us from joining that soil again
sooner rather than later
and maintain this laughable life
of red knees and red hand
praying only for the word: potato
son, don't say Pa. Potato

(time/slip)
thanks to all fornicating ancestors
whose lust imagined us

(time/slip)
How we laugh
at the pale beards, spilling out of their great boat
poles waving cloth
babbling incomprehensibly and planting
coloured cloth on a pole as if
it said something to the land
which bears the insult in silence, because it
understands law: every action has an equal
and opposite reaction. What they take from
the land will be taken from their children's children
the passenger pigeon, the tides of buffalo
the deep green hush forests they take
will be taken from their children
they are taking from themselves
too childish
to know that

(time/slip)
As the earth and sky revolve
we know not when we'll die
but this moment that recycles the past
recalculates what's to come
let us laud
the invention of Marconi
and cheese's thousand varieties
the telescope bringing the birth of stars
microscope opening the worlds we are
Jimi Hendrix wailing to all ages
with a Crybaby fuzz and lots of sustain
the pill and condom and saxophone vaccine
the birth of a nation

of movies, showing us how
time is edited by memory into flux
and stills. Praise also
a Korean monk carving backward
sutras into a block of hard-grained wood so
a whole page can print at once
Gutenberg finding true gold
in lead hot to become Gothic text

(time/plug)
Let us also laud the invention of time
most excellent illusion
because what could we have done before it
There'd be no millennial party hats
we'd have little to count on, no four/four to keep
no time to slip away
like the present
because we are born to die
let us divide life up into the most interesting units
using sixes, twelves, lunar phases
to draw the audience's eyes away from the Big One
the unit we remain in/on
tumbling towards silence and the white light
just before the power goes out
counting on one finger truth: one, zero, live, die

(time/slip)
The car landed on its side
you, because the seat belt didn't give
survived

(rime/slip)
This poem has not yet begun

we apologize for any inconvenience
yet, old bag of blood, red rover
this poem has long been over

Why bewail re-booting fate as . . .

Long Reach: Thanksgiving, 2000

For Al Purdy

In placid, willow-dragged waters
of the Long Reach
a muskrat swims on its back
human as myself on holiday
working at doing nothing: it
is just as true that I, floating on
my back, water rilling off whiskers
recall the muskrat
climbing cells shelved
in the library of my genes

As it drags Quinte Bay water along
my course makes the smallest echo
of a southbound duck flight's V

And I backswim forty years ago
when no muskrat or man
in right mind floated here
because gentlemanly Bob Hayward
in a clean white shirt and tie
was beating back Yankee hydroplanes
with beautiful *Miss Supertest*
her supercharged sixteen-cylinder Rolls-Royce Griffon
powering polished wood up to 160 mph
kicking up a rooster-tail tall as six-story
buildings that, thank God, still aren't
along the Long Reach

Now *Miss Supertest* hangs

in the Ontario Science Centre, her roar
shrunk to a single plaque, memento
mori of Bob Hayward barrel-rolling to death
on the Detroit River and
Supertest gas stations, odd little castle
keeps of the Canadian internal combustion cult
are extinct as Fina, BP, and your body from this life
Al Purdy. The mystery of how water becomes fire

Some poor, dumb, herbivorous dinosaur
two hundred million years gone reached for tender branches
just a little too far over the pond
and went in. Time cooked her down
to the high-test fuel hammering
Miss Supertest's stressed, polished pistons
rhythmic as big Canadian presses pumping
out Al Purdy poetry books
which taught me to see
timewise, my eye extending
not only the facts of the past
but the emotions that pool in a place
sung by local ghosts
buried inside the green dissembling
of goldenrod, milkweed and
caterpillars, all of them wanting

Wanting made water
spell out a nucleus, then gild it with scales
wanting inspired a fish
mocked by slimy neighbours
to go walkabout on fins
made me contemplate this
Long Reach deadhead that became

a muskrat's head examining me

Who is further along the scale
of evolving? I who want
so much in both senses – desire, and lack
this muskrat who wants nothing
and slips underwater
before I can interrogate him
Just another Hermes in a slinky fur suit
one of many messengers the world
shoves in my face, saying
"Pay attention, fool!"

It's in that silence
that the sixteen cylinders of thought
power up a rooster tail of words
call it poetry if a term is needed
or nature talking
me just the mouthpiece
a ripple on the surface
and gone

Intertexuality

The labour of being at the source
or rather, of being the source of time
is as hard as parenting wisely
and pays even more poorly

The labour of being erases
the pleasure of work
sets in its place a saddened clock
this is the source of our time
happy, sad, just bearing up
waiting for the shift to end

In art, orgasm, selfless love
may be counted the finest
evidence that the universe expands
strictly in accordance with the Big Bang theory
if energy equals mass
multiplied by the speed of light squared
if a body sufficiently removed from
other bodies
continues
in a state of rest or uniform motion then
you

The Surface of Things

We seem to be drawn on in the wake of some fast flying always disappearing black object, drawn rapidly ahead of us . . .

Virginia Woolf

Dreaming in bed, Thursday haunts
if it is, I should be teaching, not here
or is it Wednesday? The waking world
says "Monday" next, a tall man
runs up the walk, his long pole's
snagged something vague and grey
under the surface, pulls it
from a lawn's pool. I think "salmon?"
It extends fins, a lateral rainbow

These still swim in me
as I set my class to writing
an essay on violent rap lyrics
A counsellor's at the door
"Is this student present?" No
her family can't reach her
he shows me the fax: her mother
killed in Ivory Coast
my student doesn't know yet, is out there
somewhere in grey Scarborough
chasing her mother's death
something yet unseen, dark below
the surface of things

Iraq

Where artists hammer elegant bowls
of tinned copper in the suq
no deal is complete without a glass
of sweet hot tea and endless debate
where the poorest peasant is dishonoured
if you do not accept
his gift of ripe green melon
where the Tigris and Euphrates fed the creation of
Sumeria, and fresh river clay
knew the reed-ends of cuneiform writing
where men watched spinning planets
and guessed at order
where the women wail for
too many dead
where a king rode his stallion up the
spiral ramp of Samara's ziggurat
and a blind musician played his one-string rebab
under Ctesiphon's graceful blue arch

Where are there are too many antiquities
to catalogue or pick up
at Nineveh, at Ur, in the crumbling streets of Babylon
a casual kick turns up
a 3000-year-old business-letter-brick
a cruel man now reigns and in the eternal mode of despots
imprisons and murders poets
gasses children whose crime is being Kurdish
plays chess with bigger powers
sacrificing his people as pawns

Have we learned nothing since Babylon's
Hanging Gardens were green
to atttack the man must we attack
all that surrounds him
copper suks, graceful arches, wailing women,
beggars and kings' tombs
what have we learned in 5000 years except
how to throw our spear thousands of miles
its tip loaded with sharpened isotopes?
So now they say
we must attack my old Grade Six teacher
Mrs. Al-Mansoor, a laughing American woman
her offense marrying an Iraqi graduate student
We must assault the handsome taxi driver Ibrahim
who drove me to Kurdish Mosul, to reed-dwellers' Basra
so proud of his '57 Chevy
we must destroy the irrigation canals
from which my father tried to discourage the snails
who recycle bilharzia back to the poor through
the only water to drink, wash in, listen to
in this arid nation
have we learned nothing in 5000 years
except that one good attack deserves another
when the burning Bush speaks
must we obey the fires of far-righteousness
rather than our own good cool sense

Instead, drop poems on Hussein from armadas
of swans until his ears vanish
under the weight of lyrics
he the new Ozymandias
looking on our works and despairing
forget him while the suks hammer on

the one-string rebab plays
and the wind whistles through the empty bricks
of Babylon as always

Lunar

Every night, cloud rapt
chrome-dazzling
these places pass our eyes
an atlas of scars and bruises
marsh of epidemics
sea of humours
marginal sea
ocean of storms

painting the way
home for the lightless driver
the stumbling drunk
unhomed of all kinds
so at last they waver along the path to
the sea of eternity
marsh of sleep
lake of dreamers
sea of clouds

like the cold eyes of the horseman riding
by lovers lost in themselves
or lost to each other
the shining prospect opens horizons
bay of heats
sea of crises
sea of nectar
bay of rainbows

each of us has a set of moonpaths
in our coded fate, yet the

unknown places sail on
as we reach at last
that sea of waves
bay of dews
sea of vapours
lake of death

Phyllis, 1912-2002

Once you and I helped
an official Ontario bird-count
hoping to snag bugling jays
cedar-hopping chickadees, even a laconic
comic over-wintering crow
but found only pigeons
Being in country, we labelled them
more pleasingly "rock doves"
everywhere – nothing but rock doves rock doves
finally, on a barn roof blazing with the early-falling sun
another hundred rock doves
you smiled

Bird-wise now
pared to bones that sustain
flight you nestling
on your side
and we three children
ageing ourselves, watch you pace
quietly the steps
the nurse said all climb to
the door that opens pure sky

hands and feet cooling as heart
keeps only itself and the brain going
breathing soft, then intermittent
the three big breaths
on the crest of one you contract and let go
all the life force that
you've served these ninety years

and relax, your work on earth done at last
we urge you gently forth
holding your hands
don't want to let go
you release a soft breath-echo
your last quiet lesson
how to accept

When the young nurse arrives
stethoscope readied, we say
"No need. She's gone."
We should have said
flying

The Quarter Mile in Under Thirteen

He died a young man when cancer beat
him across the finishing line, but to last
he has left his '69 black Chevelle, fast
enough to bear this epitaph on its fleet
windshield: 1/4 mile in under thirteen
seconds. All this with a 350 small-block
that he taught to rev, burn rubber, walk
away with the trophies that seemed to mean
something. And now he lies at rest
his glossy trailered Chevelle, carbs and cams
cranked to infinity, sits with its Fram
oil filter forever stilled. But lest
he be neglected, his sad, gawky niece
recalls his speed, and weeps in slow peace

N-Folded

Here is enfolding, skin a carapace
wrapped around the contracting
heart set to beat slow-mo
until the sun swings close
enough again. Here is the sleeping
under layers, the sleep of no walking
until waking. Silence at the heart
of the storm. Seeds hold the tiny clocks
of their genes close. And people still abroad
hide flesh sun will not see for months
Fires are out, and the ashes' best
augury is an early end. But how beautifully
the spread shroud gleams

John Gone

On the deaths of Johnny Cash and John Ritter,
reported September 12, 2003

Two more Johns are
dead and gone
onto the list that goes on and on
of Johns that are non

Lennon at forty, new album just out
John Milton, Dryden, Keats
Dangerous John Dillinger
headless John the Baptist
John Holmes
JFK, John Barrymore, all the Kings
John, Little John, Big Bad John
John of Gaunt, of Groats
Johnny B. Goode
all gone on
and even Jeans
-Paul Sartre and Genet
all Johns done
That name worn so smooth with use
reflects the centuries of John loss
Johnlessness. Each of us finally going upstairs
with the eternal harlot lifting her veil
translating us to Johnny Angel. Or not

Johns Ritter and Cash prove
you can wear black, quench burning rings of fire
carve your hair into a standing black wave

but life won't always buy your hits
or you can milk laughs
every week on the tube
but three's a crowd, and the John goes first
while his co-star flogs Thighmasters

Someday I will go off-list
ailing of heart or lung, car or
simple time. In case no one writes me
into a poem, let me record
this John lived too, and considered
the Long John List of the Lost

Although the Dead

keep wisely silent
concerning human affairs, they cannot shake
the itch of living entirely

their translucent fingers urge colour
from the fine tips of willow
and sumac, inflate

the homely shoots becoming irises
tulips, dandelions. They code *recall*
in the muttering snowmelt

embed *return* in waves of waterbirds
arrowing down onto northern lakes
Their cells in each new cell

their ashes in the fine haze
of later-setting sun
each day this spring

Time Slip is a collection of poetry that mirrors the author's journey through time (six decades) and space (visits to the Middle East, Japan and many parts of North America). It includes selections from Oughton's first four poetry collections, plus new work written over the last ten years. The poems vary considerably in style and theme, ranging from sonnets and haiku to free-form experimentation, and considering technology, science, the nature of language itself, art, music, families, ageing, and the murky fluctuations of the human heart. The poetry is distinguished by a careful ear to the sound or words and lines, a keen and often wry sense of humour, and a celebration of the pleasures and paradoxes of existence at the beginning of the twenty-first century.

Born in Guelph, Ontario, John Oughton has traveled widely, living at various times in Iraq and Egypt, Japan, and Nova Scotia. Now based in Toronto, he is a Teaching and Learning Consultant at Centennial College. He has also worked in publishing, journalism, and corporate communications. His education includes a B.A. and M.A. in English Literature at York University (where he studied with writers including Frank Davey, Irving Layton, Eli Mandel and Miriam Waddington), doctoral work in education at OISE/University of Toronto, and non-credit writing courses at the Jack Kerouac School for Disembodied Poetics in Boulder, Colorado. He is the author of four collections of poetry, most recently *Counting Out the Millennium* (Pecan Grove Press, Texas, 1997), and close to 400 articles, reviews and interviews. He has one daughter.